A Daily Reflection:

A 32 Day Devotional Guide on Coping in Today's Society

Ann B. Rhodes

Rhodes Publishing

Hogansville, Georgia

Copyright © 2019 by **Ann B. Rhodes**

All rights reserved. No part of this publication may be reproduced, distributed, or transmitted in any form or by any means, including photocopying, recording, or other electronic or mechanical methods, without prior written permission of the publisher, except in the case of brief quotations embodied in critical reviews and certain noncommercial uses permitted by copyright law. For permission requests, write to the publisher, addressed "Attention: Permissions Coordinator," at the address below.

Ann B. Rhodes
Email address: smilingannie923@yahoo.com

Book Layout © 2019 BookDesignTemplates.com

A Daily Reflection/ Ann B. Rhodes -- 1st ed.
ISBN 978-1-7333222-0-1

Acknowledgements

This book is dedicated to God first who inspired to write this book, my family, friends, and people across the world that need extra motivation in the different things that they do in life. A lot of times life can throw you a curve ball, but you can still make it if you trust and believe in God. I hope this book is an inspiration to anyone who reads it.

"Always stop and think before reacting. The life you save could be your own."

-Ann B. Rhodes

Contents

Why did I write this?..vii
How should I speak to people?..1
What is your relationship with God?... 5
How should I raise my child?... 8
What is your secret?..12
How do I remain pure and clean?...16
Who is a true father?...19
How do I show forgiveness?... 22
Should I be concerned with people talking about me?.............. 25
How do you find out if someone is using others?...................... 28
What is your purpose in life?.. 31
How do your decisions affect everyday life?...............................34
How do you deal with the inconsistent person?........................37
What do you do with a person who has a greedy heart?............. 40
How do you know if a person is selfish?.....................................43
Can your words be used against you?.. 46
How does God feel about liars?... 49
How should a person handle anger?...53
Who can you depend on in your time of need?..........................56

Have you been touched by the Holy Spirit of God? 59

How do you finally move on and let the relationship go? 62

How do you put trust in man? 65

How do you deal with difficult people? 68

How should a person handle his finances? 71

How do you manage things when life seems
like it's falling apart? 73

Can prayer and my belief in God truly make things happen? 75

How important is it to watch what you say? 78

How difficult is it for a person to be fully faithful? 81

How should you respect your parents? 84

What is more important than food that can fill up your soul? 87

How does money change a person? 90

How do I maintain patience for the things I want? 93

Why is telling the truth so important? 96

About the Author 99

• INTRODUCTION •

Why did I write this?

I am currently being led by the Holy Spirit to stop what I am doing and write. I must write to God to thank him for blessing me and making me the person I am today. You see, when you are a child of God, the devil is going to try to knock you down. I am a living witness that if you have faith and if you believe in God, he will be your Protector, Provider, and he will make a way out of no way.

Although I am writing this during the summer of 2018, I am going to share with you through Scripture how God's word will be your spiritual food of guidance and how to make it through rough times. This devotional book will show you the Scriptures that God has laid upon my heart to express my feelings and tell the world what God has done for me through writing.

During my life, I have done things that I wanted to do, but I haven't done the things that God has wanted me to do. In order to lead a successful life, you must trust and obey God. You must think about how to give God situations and how "in fact" to leave certain situations alone. I hope this book is a true blessing to anyone who reads it. My hope is to inspire others as the Spirit of God inspired me to write this book.

DAY 1

How should I speak to people?

Proverbs 18:21-

"Death and life are in the power of the tongue: and they that love it shall eat the fruit thereof."

Have you ever stopped to think about how powerful your words truly are? One may bring up the old saying, "Sticks and stones may break my bones, but words will never hurt me." As an individual, you are in charge of your own tongue. Although people may speak hurtful words toward us, they are speaking death.

We must not allow the words of others interfere with God's word. You can either speak life out of what you say and be positive or you can speak death into your life and speak negative. You have to dream and believe that you can do anything you set your mind to.

A couple of years ago, I was actually sitting in a courtroom next to a parent who had her children taken away from her through the Department of Family and Children Services (DFACS). The mother whose children were taken away by DFACS asked, "What do you like to do?" My response, "I love to write. I'm a writer. I wrote a poetry book two years ago called *From the Beginning until Now* and I have a copy of the book with me in the courtroom. I looked through the book and found a poem titled "Walk Away" that I felt was best to read to her based on the reason why she was at court.

This mother responded to me by saying, "These are some words I need to live by." From that moment, I knew that God planted my tongue in my mouth to express the message and encouraging words that comes from him. I am so happy that God has trusted me to carry his message through poetry and other forms of writing.

Be mindful of your words and be cautious of what you speak and say to people. People listen carefully to what you say. Sometimes you find people who tell lies and constantly have to think of other ways to continue with the same lie instead of telling the truth the first time. One expression that the older people say, "What you do in the dark will come to the light". Things can be done for long periods of time both speaking and through actions, but eventually that darkness will allow one to see the light.

Words are another reflection of a person's character. Often times, we don't realize it, but we can speak things into existence. As a child, one of my biggest dreams was to write and publish a book; it took several years, but it happened. I once had an interview for a higher position and I said that I wanted to work at a bigger school and the next year it came to pass.

If you want something, you have to be determined enough to get it. Some things may seem like it will take several years to happen, but it will finally come true one day. The words you choose can either bring life or death to your well-being. Choose wisely and choose life.

One day, I received a phone call about an opportunity of a lifetime. The phone call was about a great job opportunity. From the day I graduated from college, it's something that I have always wanted to do. It is a decision that will deeply affect everything. I have to pray about the situation and weigh the pros and cons about it. The more I think about it, I look at it as an opportunity of a lifetime and I am leaning towards a new beginning. If you pray and speak something into existence, eventually, over time, it will happen.

How should I speak to people?

1. What experiences have you had with people and how they talk with you?

2. Are you choosing life with your words and being positive towards others or are you choosing death and being negative toward others?

3. How can you change your actions to make sure that you are speaking life and being positive toward yourself and others?

DAY 2

What is your relationship with God?

John 4:8-

"Draw nigh in God, and he will draw nigh to you. Cleanse your hands, ye sinners, and purify your hearts, ye double minded."

A friend once asked me the following question, "What is your relationship with God?". I paused during the phone conversation to answer. This friend told me that he was not the best person in the world so it made me think that he was thinking about his relationship with God also. If I was going to answer the question about my relationship with God, I would say I have a very strong relationship with him.

Every move I make I have to reflect upon God about the outcome. My decisions in relationships and career choices are all centered on God. If you go to God with a contrite heart, he will come closer to you, but you have to ask God in prayer for forgiveness. I told my friend that God has truly blessed me in my life. My friend said that your relationship and blessings are different.

God has blessed me on the decisions that I have made based on feedback from him. Sometimes, you have to pray and ask God for the direction to go. Sometimes, it will surprise you on how he responds. God can show you a variety of reactions and the response to things to let you know that you made the right decision about a situation or a person.

Listen to God and let the pieces fall wherever they may fall. God will give you the things that you need if you ask him. He will provide you with a car, a house, and several other things that you need. Although I had several difficulties in life growing up, God still gave me the things that I needed to be successful in life. The Lord will indeed bless you if you follow the path in him.

What is your relationship with God?

1. What is your current relationship with God?

2. What are some of the ways that you communicate with God?

3. Do you only communicate with God when you need something or do you communicate with him on a daily basis?

DAY 3

How should I raise my child?

Proverbs 22:6-

"Train up a child in the way he should go and when he is old, he will not depart from it."

I was raised in a single parent home during the 1980s. My mother worked dayshifts and nightshifts to provide for her family. Therefore, she instilled in me at an early age a strong work ethic. Our actions in life are a reflection of the type of home training we received as a child. Some people will indeed follow their upbringing while others will stray away from it, but they will always be constantly reminded of it regardless of their actions in life.

People often label me as a person who has not been around the block; I'm a good girl. I have had my share of life experiences, but everyone doesn't know about those life experiences. The only person who knows about all of my life experiences is God. I have had life flash before my eyes and God spared my life. One time, I was involved in a car accident and then, a driver was driving on the wrong side of the wrong that almost hit me. I remember saying out loud,

"Lord, have mercy!" There must be a genuine purpose of why God still has me here on Earth.

You see, when someone has had life flash before her eyes, then you change the numerous habits you have and the way you think about and approach things in life. I've learned that although one may grow up in poverty, your life experiences don't have to dictate your future circumstances. I have the experience of growing up in poverty.

I was able to set goals in my life and meet those expectations such as going to college and having a successful career. I didn't end up as a statistic as many thought that I would growing up in a life of poverty.

In order to have anything in life, you have to work for it. You can't depend on people; you have to get it done yourself. At the age of 16, I began working at the Kroger Company in order to support myself through high school and college. Although it was a struggle, my life turned out fine. I can say that my belongings God blessed me with them.

I have a successful career and I am able to provide for myself on my own. My mother taught me how to always address the elderly as well as others by saying yes or no, ma'am or sir, maintain self-control, budget, how to pray and depend on God for guidance. Now I can definitely say that my mother's training taught me respect for others, a strong work ethic, and a strong belief in God because *"I can do all things through Christ which strengthen me."* Philippians 4:13.

How should I raise my child?

1. How were you raised as a child?

2. Do you think the way you were raised made an impact on you as an adult?

3. Will the way that you were raised influence how you raise your own children?

4. What do you remember the most on how you were raised?

_____

_____

_____

_____

• DAY 4 •

What is your secret?

Philippians 3:13-

"Brethren, I count not myself to have apprehended: but this one thing I do, forgetting those things which hare behind, and reaching forth unto those things which are before."

One morning during Sunday school, we talked about what type of influence having a secret has over a person. Everyone in the world has a secret that come from bad experiences or guilt that they have never told anyone, but your secrets can actually make you sick. Be careful of the company that you keep. These people could be liars that are in your life and you might not be aware of it.

I never thought that a secret can make you sick, but depending on what type of secret it is, yes it can. Many friends of mine have told me secrets about their relationships and how it impacted the whole family. A friend shared how she had been in jail and got a lot of stuff taken away.

Someone once told me on how a person who I knew got evicted out of an apartment and had financial difficulties. I'm not the type of person that interferes with other people's affairs. I stay out of different situations. Unless it is hurting someone, I don't interfere with the deep secrets that clutter and cloud your mind.

If this one thing can clutter and cloud you mind, then it makes your judgment very foggy with your way of thinking. I've heard a friend at church say that we are only as sick as the dark secrets we keep within. I believe that a person's character speaks a lot about his or her personality and how keeping a secret can potentially bring out the worst side of a person and forces him or her to do something they will later regret in life.

All secrets represent a case of fear, self-centeredness, and a lack of ability to forget/forgive. I learned during a Sunday school lesson that when you break down the word *secrets*; it is quite interesting.

The S stands for **s**ickness. A feeling of sickness goes all over someone's body because of the guilt a person has from keeping the secret inside.

E stands for it enables us to stay stuck in the situation that we are currently in. Without getting rid of the secret, we will always feel stuck and trapped without any way of getting out.

The CR stands for confidence robbed because you no longer have the self-esteem to believe that one day you will overcome the situation. You have lost belief in one's self.

The second E stands for Evidence. You never know what evidence will be revealed because of keeping that secret. Sometimes it's easier to come clean about it.

The T stands for trust. It is hard to trust someone with a secret, but also it's hard for someone to trust you after the secret is revealed.

S stands for sink. This secret regardless of what type of secret it is could either make you sink or swim. Keeping your secrets from others could make you sink because it is eating away from you inside and it is constantly bothering you.

Do you have secrets? Are the secrets something you can share? I stated in my Sunday school class that often times, you have to go to God in your secret closet, tell the secret to God, and then just leave it alone. Let God handle the situation and work it out. Although that seems tough, God is above every situation and he handles things on his end.

What is your secret?

1. What is a big secret that you have kept?

2. How would this secret effect everyone if it was revealed?

3. Have you thought about sharing this secret with God in your secret closet?

DAY 5

How do I remain pure and clean?

Ephesians 5:3-4-

*3 "But fornication, and all uncleanness or covetousness,
Let it not be once named among you, become saints."*

*4 "Neither filthiness, nor foolish talking, nor jesting,
which are not convenient: but rather giving of thanks."*

Fornication is a sin that over half of the people in the United States are in guilty of. A coworker once told me why buy the cow, when you can get the milk for free. That's a concept that the majority of America has decided to follow. Some people are Christians and some are not. I am not here to judge anyone, but we all need to remember that our bodies are a temple of God. We must take care of our bodies because our bodies will not last forever. In your life, it is natural to have fun and enjoy yourself, but at what cost?

If you know that some of your actions present a problem, then simply stop some of those actions. This sin could include people who are married or who are in other relationships being involved with other people in a different relationship. If you involved with someone else and you are talking to another person like you are in a relationship with him or her is wrong within the eyes of God.

Anything that's truly important is worth waiting for. A lot of times women get caught up in the idea of falling in love and they are not really in love. Instead, they are only going through the motions and trying to fill a void that is missing from their life. Females take notice.

If a man truly cares for you and wants to be with you, he will honor and respect you. If a man is serious about you, he will not let anything or anyone stop him from being with you. Conversations will be filled with how to make a life together and be successful.

Be patient and God will send you a soul mate when you least expect it. Be wary of men who are very biblical with Scriptures and full of fornication in the same conversations. Who really has their priorities straight? They are the same ones who hide the other relationships he is currently involved while trying to be with you at the same time. Sometimes husbands and wives decide to fornicate outside of their marriage due to unhappiness and because they have never been able to commit to one person.

How do I remain pure and clean?

1. In our society, is it hard to remain pure and clean in a relationship? Why do you think so?

2. How do you truly know if this relationship is going to develop into something more?

3. How much do you involve God in your relationship in order to stay pure and clean?

• DAY 6 •

Who is a true father?

Psalm 68:5-

"A father of the fatherless, and a judge of the widow, is God in his holy habitation."

I have always heard one say that anyone can be a father, but it takes a special person to be a dad. Topics like this are very sensitive to me because I myself was raised in a single parent home. I have often dreamed of going to different places with my dad, but it simply didn't happen. I tried establishing a relationship with my father at a young age, but the relationship failed between my father and me. I desperately wanted to be involved in his life.

In fact, I wrote a poem about it in my book From the Beginning Until Now called: "Facing My Reality". A lot of men don't put God first, family second, and themselves last. Often times, men think about women and their romantic relationships before thinking about their child. Many men fail to realize a child will be by your side when that love you thought you had has found someone else. A man should spend as much time as possible with his child especially if he is not with the child's mother.

Don't let the relationship with the mother affect the type of relationship you have with your child, your own flesh and blood. An innocent child didn't ask to be brought into this world. If you can't be there for your children, think twice about having them. I think, often times, men don't think about the consequences of their actions with women.

If you have a child out of wedlock, ultimately the mother is going to be the main one raising the child. Very seldom do you have a man who is going to step up to the plate and be a true father without being married to the mother.

Some men look at it as a burden that has been placed upon them after the child has been born. The man should have thought about all of the responsibilities in the time of his sexual decision.

Who is a true father?

1. Did you have the opportunity to be raised up with your father?

2. How did the relationship with your father affect you as an adult?

3. Did your relationship with your father affect how you view someone who you are involved in a relationship with?

DAY 7

How do I show forgiveness?

Matthew 6:14-15-

14 "For if ye forgive men their trespasses, your heavenly Father will also forgive you."

15 "But if ye forgive not men their trespasses, neither will your father forgive your trespasses."

The golden rule is "Do unto others as you want them to do until you." Often times, if a person has treated you wrong, you want to act exactly how they have acted towards you. Is this the right way to act towards them? No, regardless of the way a person has treated you, you have to find it in your heart to forgive them.

I remember a couple of years ago, I told someone something in confidence and about a week later I heard the same exact thing I said from another person. This experience taught me a couple of things. Be very cautious of people you share things with. You can't trust everyone when you tell them different things. If you want something repeated, only share that information. It took me a long time to forgive this person, but I knew that it was something that

I needed to do. However, I did not tell this person anything else. I learned rapidly that this person was not trustworthy at all. I never sit down with the person to officially resolve the issue. From that day forward, I told my family members important information only.

So, therefore, going forward I learned how to deal with that person in a very limited way. Often times, you have to be put in situations like that to learn a lesson and how to forgive. When I forgive someone, I have to really have a talk with God to seek guidance of what to do and how to handle the situation. I pray the following prayer.

Dear Heavenly Father,
Give me strength,
In order for me to live my day,
Although I don't know how to react
Please guide me and show me the way.
Several people have hurt me,
But I need to learn how to walk away,
I had to forgive them,
So, I can receive peace from it each day.
Lord I ask you to guide me as I forgive each person,
As I repent for my own sins,
Thank –you Lord for forgiving me,
And making the sacrifice for me to live.

How do I show forgiveness?

1. Have you forgiven everyone that you need to in order to have a stronger relationship with God?

2. Name something that someone who you thought was your friend did to you that made it very hard to forgive them.

3. What are the different things that you had to do in order to forgive that person? Did you completely forget about the situation?

• DAY 8 •

Should I be concerned with people talking about me?

Proverbs 22:6-

"Train up a child in the way he should go and when he is old, he will not depart from it."

If you are a true believer in God, regardless of what people do to you, you will always succeed. When I pray to God and put my trust in him, then he will bless me with the things that I need. Although I had to work hard to achieve all of my dreams, it was well worth it in the end.

I had to work hard in high school academically, get a part-time job while I was in high school to help pay for college. I might not always get things when I want them, but I would always get them on time.

I remember when I was 14 years old, I was told that if I didn't get scholarships that I would not be attending college. Although I grew up in a single parent home in poverty, my mother provided for my brothers and me. She taught me that if you want to have something you have to get out there and work for it. I got a job at the local McDonald's at home and worked there for around six months. I went to the next city over and got a job at Kroger. At Kroger, I was a cashier, a floor supervisor, worked in customer service, and finished my employment working in the pharmacy. I was able to work through my college years at Kroger. I worked days, nights, evenings, and weekends to get where I am today.

Regardless of the negativity and the people saying I would end up getting pregnant out of wedlock, I went on to earn a Bachelor of Arts degree in Early Childhood education, a Masters and Specialist in Elementary Education, an add-on in Educational Leadership, and a Gifted in Field endorsement certification. I attended a private college in a small city and I currently have a successful teaching career.

I didn't allow the words that were spoken against me hurt me in the long run. I'm not married and have never had children, yet I have taken care of over at least fifty foster children in my home. I am a living witness that if you believe in him that you can do everything through him and God will continue to bless you even more.

Should I be concerned with people talking about me?

1. How much does it truly bother you on what people say about you?

2. Have you ever confronted someone who has said something to you? How did that conversation go?

3. Have you prayed for the person instead that talked about you? What all did you say in your prayer? Write a prayer in the space below.

• DAY 9 •

How do you find out if someone is using others?

Luke 8:17-

"For all that is secret will eventually be brought into the open, and everything that is concealed will be brought to light and made known to all."

Have you ever heard of the saying "What goes around comes around?". It is a saying that people must take to their heart. A lot of people wonder why they are having bad luck, all the time, but one must stop and ask themselves, "How am I treating others?". I knew a person who had a friend named Lisa who never told her the truth. Rachel was always willing to listen and even let the person borrow some money without any questions asked. Lisa would always tell Rachel they made more money than her. If that was the case, why borrow money from someone in the first place? Then when Rachel asked for the money back, the relationship went downhill. Rachel was able to see the borrower's true colors come out. Talk is always cheap. The money was paid back, but reluctantly. Watch people who are always inconsistent.

A conversation may go one way on Monday and another way on Tuesday. Always be mindful of what you say to others. You never know when someone might be secretly recording you. It's the same difference with having a mate.

If a significant other is in a committed relationship to one person and talking to another person, is the other person being used? How can someone talk biblical and religiously when he or she is participating in sin? It's easy for some but it's difficult for others, but if you are using someone eventually it's going to catch up with you. Remember what is done in the dark will always come out to the light.

How do you find out if someone is using others?

1. Have you ever felt that someone has used you before?

2. Has anyone ever lied to you consistently? Did the person know that you were aware of the lie? How did you handle the situation?

3. Is it better to sit back and watch a person who doesn't tell the truth or is it better to confront them about the situation?

• DAY 10 •

What is your purpose in life?

Ephesians 2:10-

"For we are his workmanship, created in Christ Jesus unto good workmanship, created in Christ Jesus unto good works, which God hath before ordained that we should walk in them."

Sometimes I have to stop and think am I using my time and talents to truly fulfill my God-given purpose? As an eight-year-old, I started writing, but I never discovered the talent until I was in middle school. When I truly discovered my talent, I was able to publish my writing in newspapers, on the internet, and even at a television station. The special gift that God has blessed me with is the ability to write poetry. I didn't realize my gift of writing until the Lord led me to put all of my writing together to publish a book as an adult. I have always been led to keep a journal and notebooks with all of my poems in it. I was able to type all of my poems and submit them to a publishing company.

Although the devil tried to prevent that from happening, it still did not work. My book was published anyway, regardless of the obstacles, I had to face because God wanted me to spread his message. You see, when you are a child of God, obstacles will come your way, but they will not be strong enough to truly block you. The different messages God wanted me to send to his people continues even today. I will proudly honor God's request by being his servant in what he wants me to do. So, I stop to ask you, what's your gift? What's your purpose in life?

What is your purpose in life?

1. What do you think your purpose in life is?

   _____
   _____
   _____
   _____

2. Have you tried to discover your gift?

   _____
   _____
   _____
   _____

3. How has the devil tried to block you from your purpose or your blessings in life?

   _____
   _____
   _____
   _____

• DAY 11 •

How do your decisions affect everyday life?

Deuteronomy 30:19-

"I call heaven and earth to record this day against you, that I have set before you life and death, blessing and cursing, therefore choose life, that both thou and thy seed may live."

Life is all about choices. In life, you will encounter blessings and a cursing, prosperity and poverty, health and sickness, and joys and sorrows, but it's up to you as an individual on how you handle it. Whatever decision you make will determine your destination and path in life. The decisions you make will determine your success or your failures.

I asked someone one time, "What are you plans for the day?". His reply was, "I don't know. I don't plan my day out". I really don't plan my day out either, but I have an idea if I am going to cook, clean, wash, or go to the store because I need something. If I didn't get finished with a project from the day before, I know I need to work on it the next day. Some people are impulsive and they live on the edge each day. They have no idea of how they got themselves in the situation they are currently in until the person who doesn't plan out the day would actually stop and think about it.

How do you make your decisions? Do you make your decisions based on what is said from a television show, a friend, a relative, family members, or the Holy Bible? Depending on who influences you with your decisions will determine the destination or path that you go in life. As hard as it was for me to do it, eventually, I had to let that friendship go in order to prosper and grow. As a person, you must accept the consequences of the decisions you've made. The decisions you make in your earthly home determines your destination in your eternal home.

Do you want to go to heaven or hell? That is the most important decision that you can make in your lifetime.

How do your decisions affect your everyday life?

1. What type of decisions have you made throughout the years that have affected your everyday life?

2. How do you make the various decisions in your life?

3. Will the decisions that you have made get you into heaven or hell? Have you prayed for forgiveness of your sins to God?

• DAY 12 •

How do you deal with the inconsistent person?

Matthew 23:3-

"All therefore whatsoever they bid you observe, that observe and do, but do not ye after their works for they say, and do not."

This Scripture represents the person who says that he will do things and in fact will never follow through with what he has promised you.

Everyone has to be cautious of the friends he/she keeps, but particularly of the ones who makes promises. I'll start off with an example: Jordan told Kendrick that he would help him with his science project. Kendrick was very excited about it and even told some of his coworkers about it. At the last minute, Jordan decided not to help his friend with it. Kendrick was glad that a date had not been set for the project and nothing had been organized yet. He thought about it for a while and decided that it was actually something that he could have done for himself, but this person said, "I will help you out anyway that I can". Again, the help never came through.

Kendrick got tired of waiting and made time to do it himself. You see, never volunteer to help someone if you can't follow through with the help.

Sometimes, you ask people to do small tasks to just to see their reaction before you ask something major. In hindsight, when a person is in need, I help with no questions asked.

I am a living witness that actions speak louder than words. A person will show their true character from the way they act. Talk is cheap, but actions from a person will definitely make a difference.

How do you deal with an inconsistent person?

1. As you deal with different people throughout your life, how do you deal with a person who is inconsistent?

2. Have you ever had a person who made a promise to you that he or she did not keep? How did you handle it?

3. How should you deal with a person like this moving forward?

• DAY 13 •

What do you do with a person who has a greedy heart?

Proverbs 1:19-

"So the ways of everyone that is greedy of gain, which taketh away the life of the way of the owners there of."

Has anyone ever referred to you as greedy? Why would someone make a statement like that at all? The definition of greedy is being selfish for the desire of something in wealth or power. Some people who often try to get everything in the world are often labeled as greedy.

They sometimes have the traits of being very demanding. People who are often greedy tend to lose everything he has.

I remember a neighbor saw that someone had bought a new car. That neighbor saw the new silver Honda Accord with a sunroof and leather seats and decided to buy the same car, but her car was a different color. Instead of her looking at the financial status of one's self, she wanted to copy off of the other person. After a couple of months, the car went back to the dealership. We have to remember to live within our own means and do whatever we are able to do.

If I see someone out there helping themselves by getting a job, paying their bills, and going to school, well, I am proud of them. I can only worry about what is going to be good for myself and my family.

What do you do with a person who has a greedy heart?

1. How do you deal with a person who has a greedy heart?

2. Is it difficult to be friends with a person who has a greedy heart?

3. Have you ever had a person to copy off of you for something you bought or an action you did only to lose it in the end? Explain that situation and how it turned out.

DAY 14

How do you know if a person is selfish?

James 3:16-

"For where envying and strife is, there is confusion and every evil work."

Anytime you find jealousy and selfishness from people, it always causes trouble. You will find out that people fall into different categories of selfishness. A person is selfish when he only thinks about themselves.

For example, if you are a teacher and you are using a resource that's beneficial to your students and you don't share it with another coworker, is that being selfish?

Every situation is different. So, in each case you have to be very cautious. You have to see if the person is able to help themselves first because if not, someone is trying to take advantage of you. I remember a long time ago I asked someone to be a mentor for me. This person helped me, but because of being selfish I was able to see first-hand how someone could "stab me in the back". It happened a couple of months later, but I was able to drop down on my knees and pray for the person who they did me wrong.

The most important thing is that I was able to forgive her for her actions through my prayers and talks with God.

How do you know if a person is selfish?

1. Have you ever had to deal with a very selfish person? Explain the situation that you had to deal with them.

2. Reflecting back on that situation, how would you have handled the situation differently?

3. Moving forward, how do you plan to interact with selfish people?

DAY 15

Can your words be used against you?

James 3:8-

"But the tongue can no man tame, it is an unruly evil full of deadly poison."

Now read this scripture again: "But the tongue can no man tame, it is an unruly evil full of deadly poison". Have you often said things that you didn't realize at the time, that you wished that you could take back after you said them? That is where this Scripture is coming from. Often times, we say things that are hurtful and spiteful that can cause harm to another human being. Your mouth can control your tongue in all situations. Sometimes your own mouth can speak things into existence.

As the saying goes, you have to be careful on what you say because it can come to pass. I remember saying that I wanted to work in a bigger school setting with more teachers and students. A couple of months later, it in fact happened. I realized how much I miss working in a smaller school setting with less teachers and students. Your words are very powerful.

Another example of how deadly your words are, send an email or a text message. An email or a text is definitely something you can't erase and it can stick with you for long periods of time. If you include a description of a situation that you sent to the wrong person, then you can get in trouble for sending the email to the wrong person.

Once you have something in writing, it can follow you for a lifetime. Make sure that you are careful on how you treat people and talk about people with your words. The very one you talk about and mistreat is the one that you might need years down the road.

Although the person may have forgiven you of the situation, they can always remind you of what happened years ago and not give you any help at all.

Can your words be used against you?

1. Have you ever said something that you have regretted? How did you try to rectify the situation?

2. Have you ever said something that you wanted and it happened? How did you feel after it actually came into existence?

3. How will you start using your words differently?

• DAY 16 •

How does God feel about liars?

Psalms 5:6-

*"Thou shalt destroy them that speak leasing:
The Lord will abhor the bloody deceitful man."*

Psalm 101:7

*"He that worketh deceit shall not dwell within my house:
he that telleth lies shall not tarry in my sight."*

Liars will be destroyed by the Lord because the Lord despises the people who tells lies and then cover it up with another lie. These people show how untrustworthy they are by the deceitful lies out of their mouth. Remember that any deceitful person will not live in the kingdom of God. Liars are not welcome into heaven. When a person is a liar then he is deceitful and untrustworthy.

I knew a lady that told lies to everyone she came in contact with. A lot of the people she lied to actually corresponded with each other and figured out she was telling lies. This lady once told someone that she went to church one particular Sunday with me. This was a false statement because I didn't go to church the particular Sunday that was mentioned.

One time there was a lady in need who needed to borrow some money. Having a loving heart, I let the lady borrow a couple of dollars. I found out that she told a different story to someone else to get more money. I lost trust in that particular individual. I found out quickly that she didn't appreciate the good help that she had.

My best friend had a guy who was a habitual liar to her. The guy she was talking to was not happy in his current love relationship but he decided to get involved with another female. He made sure that neither woman would find out about each other. In essence, he was actually fooling around with two different women. Instead of the guy just being truthful and saying that he was seriously involved with his current girlfriend, not just saying that his heart wasn't free would have been more of an honest answer.

My friend knew that he was involved with someone where he was currently living. The guy should have said that he wanted to see how things was going to work out between him and his current girlfriend. Instead, he would always say, "Let's be just friends!".

Although he would say that particular phrase, he was still cheating on his current girlfriend, but it was fine in his eyes because the two of them were not married. If the two of them were married, would he still cheat and be a liar?

Although he knew fornication was wrong, he would still commit the act with his girlfriend he was dating and the woman he wasn't married. He did a great job lying to both although he spent more time with the girlfriend than the other woman. The lies actually got stronger that they started contradicting themselves on what he had just said the week before. The lies got more interesting and deeper with each conversation that eventually the conversations began to get shorter and shorter.

Instead of talking to each other each day, it led to every other day, then a couple of times a week, then every once in a while. When a person tells a lie, he or she has to tell another lie to make the first lie stand. Then sometimes the person has forgotten about the first lie that was told so the next lie contradicts what was said and you finally find out that the person isn't trustworthy.

Regardless of how much pain might be caused, it's better to always tell the truth in the beginning. More respect is given when you are truthful and honest, then you don't have to worry about the consequences that will happen later on when you tell the truth.

How does God feel about liars?

1. How do you think that God feels about liars?

   _____
   _____
   _____
   _____

2. Has someone ever lied to you and you found that he/she was telling a lie? How did that make you feel toward that person?

   _____
   _____
   _____
   _____

3. How should you deal with a person who always tell lies?

   _____
   _____
   _____
   _____

• DAY 17 •

How should a person handle anger?

Proverbs 15:1-

"A soft answer turneth away wrath: but grievous words stir up anger."

What is the proper way to act when a person gets angry? Everyone acts different when he gets angry. Some people yell or throw things, some people use profanity, while others have the ability to remain calm. The question is: What is the best way to handle anger?

According to the Bible, one should remain calm in order to turn away trouble. It's another lesson concerning how to control your tongue. Your words can break you or destroy you. I remember a lady whom I worked with once said grievous words toward me in order to make me angry and to make me say some words that I should not say.

I remember talking to God at that particular moment in order to stay calm and felt a person that I had a lot of respect for really betrayed me. It took a lot for me to finally forgive that person, but I did. Sometimes, people will get you mad just to see what type of reaction you will have.

Don't let the enemies win. As the old saying goes, kill them with kindness. Never let another person get under your skin.

How should a person handle anger?

1. What are some different things that you do or reactions that you have when you get mad?

2. How should you handle your anger?

3. How do you forgive the person who made you angry?

• DAY 18 •

Who can you depend on in your time of need?

Matthew 25:35-

"For I was hungered, an ye gave me meat: I was thirsty, and ye gave me drink: I was a stranger, and ye took me in."

I heard my grandmother talk about how difficult things were during the time when she was growing up. Although my grandmother didn't live during the world wars, I really think that some people would have a very difficult time being alive during that time period. Let me give an example of the mighty God that we serve.

On a hot summer night, my grandmother was walking to the store because she had no food at home and none of her relatives would provide her with a meal. She was weak and she was tired, but she was determined to find something to eat. As she was walking in the hot sun, she stopped on the side of the road, dropped down on her knees, and began to pray. She asked God to feed her since others had turned their backs on her. She fell down on the side of the road asking God for his help. When she got up, she was full as if she had just eaten a full meal. God had just fed my grandmother through the Spirit. God will supply your every need if you just ask him.

An old coworker of mine that I worked with at Kroger years ago lost her new manager job that she just got. She had a family to support, but she had absolutely no income. Without any income, she couldn't pay her mortgage nor put food on the table for her or her children. The only thing that helped to save her was her belief in God and the power of prayer. When one door closed, another door opened up for a job opportunity.

Always keep your hands in God's unchanging hands. He will come in and make a way out of no way if you follow his commandments.

Who can you depend on in your time of need?

1. Who can you truly depend on when you need help?

2. Has anyone tried to help you that you actually helped when they needed?

3. Do you have trust for the people you depend on or are you very cautious on the people that might help you?

• DAY 19 •

Have you been touched by the Holy Spirit of God?

Romans 15:13-

"Now the God of hope fill you with all joy and peace in believing, that ye may abound in hope, through the power of the Holy Ghost."

If you have experienced the power of the Holy Ghost that comes inside of you, you know that it is a very unique feeling that you have. I've had that experience before in my life.

At the beginning of the new year, a former coworker of mine contacted me on Facebook messenger to invite me to come to her church the next Sunday for a musical ministry. I am so glad I was able to go on that particular Sunday. The previous year had been a struggle in my career. I had to change schools, therefore, I had to learn rules and procedures all over again. So, I definitely wanted this new year to be a better one. The service began with prayer and worship. A guest musician came in.

I can definitely say that the Holy Spirit filled the room. The guest played a powerful song in the musical ministry called "Break Every

Chain". The previous month I had a bad experience with some people talking bad about me. This song did something to my soul. I cannot describe the feeling that went through my body, but it was electric. To hear this particular song did something to my soul because this is the first time ever that I began crying. The Lord touch me in a way that I've never been touched before.

After the song "Breakthrough" started playing, I knew the Holy Spirit hit me. I knew that everything was going to be just fine. When you have the power of God on your side, whom shall I fear, whom shall I be afraid? At this point, I knew that I should continue focusing on God's words and spreading his message through the worldly things filled through the world.

Have you been touched by the Holy Spirit of God?

1. Have you ever been touched by the Holy Spirit of God? How did it make you feel?

2. If you have been touched by the Holy Spirit, did it make you look at things differently?

3. How does your belief in God make you look at people, view the world, and act toward things differently?

• DAY 20 •

How do you finally move on and let the relationship go?

John 14:27-

"Peace I leave with you; my peace I give to you. Let not your hearts be troubled, neither let them be afraid."

Regardless of how much you may love and still care for a person, sometimes, it's best to let them completely go because in the times of adversity and in the time of trouble, you can definitely see what a person's true character is. Love is a beautiful thing, but at the same time, love can also hurt you.

A friend of mine dated a guy for a couple of years and over time the relationship fell apart. Several years down the road, the two hooked back up through social media. He was with another girl at the time, but he still decided to communicate with my friend. He even came to see my friend a couple of times—in essence, cheating. Whenever him and his current girlfriend had some type of falling out, disagreement, or argument, he would come and visit my friend.

For some reason, he wanted to get married to my friend without presenting a ring, asking the father for his daughter's hand in marriage, or even getting down on one knee. My friend was very level headed, and all she really wanted was to sit down and talk to him to come up with a plan to see if they could truly make it work. My friend's plan was to date for a little while, get engaged, then get married, but the guy wasn't hearing that at all. He wanted to have a baby on top of everything else.

My friend wanted to make sure that their concepts and values were the same before bringing an innocent child into the world and being irrational by getting married. After a couple of months, the guy finally backed off and went back to pursuing his current relationship that he was not happy in.

Although my friend never said no, this guy acted as if time was against him. My friend had to let go of the whole situation and move on. If it's truly meant to be, it will all work out. At this point, my friend knows that God will mend her broken heart. She never wanted to get her feelings and emotions involved in the situation at all.

The guy eventually stopped calling and texting without any warning because he is still confused and feels rejected from a couple of months ago. If he would have went about it in a more patient way instead of trying to rush everything my friend would have been married by now.

How do you finally move on and let the relationship go?

1. How do you finally move on and let a relationship go?

2. How difficult is it to finally let things go? Will you get tangled up in the situation again?

3. What are some things that you need to do in order to let a relationship truly go and never look back on it again?

• DAY 21 •

How do you put trust in man?

Psalm 118:8-

"It is better to take refuge in the Lord than to trust man."

When it comes to trust, who is the only person who you can trust? God is the only person you can trust. Adults have the syndrome to run and tell everything someone tells them. When you tell one person something, pretty soon the entire workforce knows about it or even the entire community. If you don't want any secrets repeated, trust in God always, don't trust in man.

My friend once told me there was a guy that she told all of her secrets. She shared with him things that she has never shared with other people. This guy played with her emotions, used her, and eventually stopped talking to her. Although he may never tell anyone any of those secrets, there still is a big trust issue there. He wanted to know everything about her, but yet and still he was never truthful to her. He never told her the financial situation he was truly in with detail or that he had been evicted out of a house and an apartment before. He would always say that God will provide, and yes, he will. But God also gives one knowledge and common sense to help one survive in the world.

Some people make decisions based on impulse without thinking of the consequences of his actions. Never tell people or give people information because they have the power over you. Again, have your faith and trust in God and not in man at all. Man lacks the knowledge and understanding and use of all the information in the years to come.

How do you put trust in man?

1. Is it wise to trust your fellow man with personal things that you have to share?

2. Is it better to share things with God and go into your secret closet to talk to him?

3. Why do you put so must trust in man instead of putting all of our trust in God?

• DAY 22 •

How do you deal with difficult people?

Luke 6:27-28-

27 "But I say unto you which hear, Love your enemies, do good to them which hate you."

28 "Bless them that curse you, and pray for them which despitefully use you."

It's hard for you to act nice to a person who may have used profanity toward you or betrayed you in some type of way. A person's tongue is the ultimate controller in situations. Often times, when you have that coworker or best friend stab you in the back, it's hard to let go of certain things. But according to Scripture, let situations like that go. Love the people who have betrayed you and done you wrong.

I remember when I was younger how my friends would get on the phone and get on three-way with each other to see if someone was talking about them without them knowing someone else was on the phone. Years ago, we didn't have caller ID. Sometimes,

I could hear people talk about me like I was a dog. These same people knew how to smile in my face at the same time.

You always have to be mindful of what you say around people. You never know how a person actually feels about you. As my mother would say, "A shut mouth will go a long way". It's better to keep your mouth closed and listen than to comment on a situation. I use the philosophy of kill them with kindness. Love people regardless of how they treat you. You will reap what you sow. The very person who did you wrong will get what he readily deserves in the end.

How do you deal with difficult people?

1. What is the best way to deal with difficult people?

2. How do you deal with the people that you know talk behind your back?

3. Would you still help a person who you know has talked about you and did you wrong if they were in a time of need?

DAY 23

How should a person handle his finances?

Philippians 4:19-

"But my God shall supply all your need according to his riches in glory by Christ Jesus."

The type of job you have and your lifestyle preferences play a big role in your finances. As a child, I grew up in poverty. I was poor and I was raised up in a single parent home. My mother had a job to make ends meet and to support her family. Regardless, if my mother worked day or night, she made sure her family was well taken care of. The income she had wasn't much, but she made sure her children had a roof over their head and food on the table. She planted the seed in her children to do well in school and to get an education. So, her children were able to be successful. She wanted her children to have a better job than she did.

When we get into a financial crunch, we must allow God to direct our finances. It goes back to that needs versus wants phenomenon. Normally, people run into problems financially when they tend to spend on what he wants verses what God means for him to have with his funds.

How should a person handle his finances?

1. How should a person handle his finances?

2. Depending on how often you get paid, do you have a budget that you set for yourself?

3. Do you have money set aside that you only touch in case of emergencies?

• DAY 24 •

How do you manage things when life seems like it's falling apart?

Zephaniah 3:17-

"The Lord thy God in the midst of thee is mighty; he will save, he will rejoice over thee with joy; he will rest in love, he will joy over thee with singing."

Sometimes in life, it seems like your whole word is falling apart, but you have to keep the faith and believe in God. God and his angels are always with you. God is with you through sickness, and he can heal you if it's his will. God is in control of circumstances, so you have to always trust in him even when things are going rough.

Sometimes people step out on faith in terms of jobs due to their strong belief in God.

I remember a coworker quit her job at the end of the year and she had nothing else lined up. She prayed and asked God for guidance. She stepped out on faith and the Lord blessed her with a job that was closer to home. Though it seems her income is lower, she is happier. This is one of many proofs that God is always with you and always preparing something better.

How do you manage things when everything seems like it's falling apart?

1. How do you manage things when everything seems like it's falling apart?

2. When your stress level is high, what are some things that you do in order to relieve stress?

3. Do you tend to lean on God more when you are stressed or do you depend more on man?

• DAY 25 •

Can prayer and my belief in God truly make things happen?

Luke 1:37-

"For with God nothing shall be impossible."

1 John 5:14-

"And this is the confidence that we have in him, that, if we ask anything according to his will, he heareth us."

I have always heard my pastor say that prayers change things. From listening to different people and from personal experience, I pray each day. The power of prayer is the strongest spiritual connection to God that you can have.

A friend once told me that he lost contact with a girl that he had in mind to marry one day. The guy said that he had prayed for years to one day get back together. The guy had moved away years ago, so both parties lived in different areas. One day in the area of business on his way back, he rode past the area of where the girl lived when they dated years ago. He decided not to stop because he didn't feel it was the right time. He continued to pray so one day the girl contacted him through social media and they started talking on the phone again. It was like they never missed a beat. Prayer brought two people back into each other's lives.

I know a young man who recently finished college trying to find a job in his profession. Although he did fairly well, one person who didn't give him a good reference kept him from a job. This young man believed in God and didn't let that stop him. He decided to go back to the drawing board and take a certification test. He passed the certification test and it opened up many doors. I am pleased to say this young man got a teaching job.

You see, when you are a child of God "No weapon formed against me shall prosper". The odds seemed like they were against this young man, but prayer truly changed things in that situation.

Can prayer and my belief in God truly make things happen?

1. How much do you really believe in the power of prayer?

2. Do you believe that if you pray for something that eventually you will get what you prayed for?

3. What do you when you continue to pray and nothing happens?

• DAY 26 •

How important is it to watch what you say?

Proverbs 13:3-

"He that keepeth his mouth keepeth his life: but he that openeth wide his lips shall have destruction."

In today's society, you have to be very careful of what you say around people. People can use your words against you. Even if you have told someone something in confidence, one day, all of those conversations can eventually come back and be used to overpower you.

There was once a guy who said he wanted marriage one day, but had a difficult time expressing how he really felt. He would never sit-down face to face with the person and really talk about the aspects of taking that big step. The girl finally decided to keep her mouth shut to watch and observe. It was amazing to see the concept "actions speak louder than words" fully develop. The only request the female had was to date, get engaged, and then get married. Evidently, the guy wasn't satisfied with following those steps. The girl began to keep her mouth shut just to see what was really going on.

True colors came to light and only a friendship could continue between the two of them. The male struggled in life more than the female simply because his lips and actions had brought plenty of destruction in his lifetime. Unless he wanted to make some serious changes, his life was going to continue in the direction it was headed in.

How important is it to watch what you say?

1. How important is it to watch what you say?

2. Have the different things that you have said to people ever got you into trouble or caused chaos in your life?

3. How can watching what a person says determine a lot about their character?

• DAY 27 •

How difficult is it for a person to be fully faithful?

Proverbs 28:20-

"A faithful man shall abound with blessings, but he that maketh haste to be rich shall not be innocent."

In today's society, it becomes more and more difficult for couples to be faithful to each other. On Facebook and Instagram, a person can easily send a private message to someone and only the two of them would know about it. These social media accounts are password protected so it's more difficult for the significant other to find out cheating is going on in a relationship. It's very rare that a lot of people are really involved in a committed relationship.

For example, if you've dated someone for years and even if an old ex-lover comes back in the picture, do you start thinking about what could have been? Some guys will be involved in a relationship, but still talk to other females. Communication with these other females could be through telephone conversations, text messages, or social media. You may go visit them every once in and while, but you are still involved in the other relationship. You think marriage is the way out, but why didn't you marry the partner you are currently with? When this other person finally starts to come around, then the guy starts to instantly back away. Is it because he realized it was wrong to continue to have a love triangle? Was the guy running away from something that went wrong in the current relationship at the time?

As the old saying goes, never start anything you can't finish. People's hearts and feelings get tied up into the situation. If you want to be in a relationship with someone, make sure it's only them. If you are married, don't invite others over to your house-even if you know your spouse will not be at home. If you are not happy in a relationship, then get out of it, but be a faithful person in the relationship.

If you can't be faithful to all parties involved then don't be in a relationship. That way, no one gets hurt and you don't have to cover up conversations with lies and have a guilty conscience trying to hide something.

How difficult is it for a person to be fully faithful?

1. Is it hard for you to commit yourself in a relationship?

2. How important do you think communication is in order to keep a faithful relationship?

3. If you are aware of the past of a significant other and he was unaware that you knew, would you ever tell him the truth? Why or why not?

• DAY 28 •

How should you respect your parents?

Exodus 20:12-

"Honour thy father and thy mother; that thy days may be long upon the land which the Lord thy God giveth thee."

Children are more social and active in this generation. As I was raised back during the 80's, I was taught to respect my elders and to reply by saying, "Yes, ma'am" and "No, ma'am" or "Yes, sir and No, sir". If your mother told you to do something, then you had to do it with no questions asked. Regardless of how you may have felt about doing things. I did not back talk my mother or disrespect her. I knew the consequences if that occurred. It was powerful for me as a child to have to pick out my own "switch" outside. I learned the correct way I should act like a child with manners and respect. It's a new generation of children in our society now.

Children talk back, disobey, and do what they want to do. As the old folks would say, these children have started to smell themselves. Children disrespect not only their own parents, but school officials as well. This generation doesn't realize that all of the disrespect that they are displaying is only making their days on Earth shorter.

Many children fail to go to church and fully understand the biblical teachings of God. I hope and pray that this generation finds the right path to God.

I know a child who lived with her grandmother and the grandmother asked the little girl to clean out the tub. The little girl replied to the grandmother, "I'm not the only one who uses the tub." Instead of just cleaning out the tub, she had to give a smart comment back not realizing that her days will be shorten by not honoring the elderly. Be careful and respect the elderly, regardless of how you may feel.

How should you respect your parents?

1. How should you respect your parents?

2. What are some ways that you show your children on how to respect their elders?

3. What can be done in a child's young age to teach them the importance of respecting adults and follow the direction of what they say?

• DAY 29 •

What is more important than food that can fill up your soul?

Proverbs 119:103-

"How sweet are thy words unto taste: Yea, sweeter than honey to my mouth."

How often do we read the Bible to receive our spiritual food? Just like we have to eat regular food to stay alive, we need our spiritual food to renew our bodies and souls. In order to grow spiritually in the Lord, we must read our Bibles, go to church, go to Sunday school, go to Bible Study, and simply meditate on God's word. It's a lot of things such as the parables found in the Bible that are currently happening in the world that has already been stated in the Bible.

If people truly read the Bible, people can read how to solve the storms of people's problems and how these storms occur. It's a sign from God that people need to get saved and begin doing right by him. Look at how things are for a believer versus a non-believer and how things change for the people who finally become saved and stop all of those sinful acts.

Blessings comes in a variety of ways which include a blessing in a house, car, or job promotion.

What is more important than spiritual food that can fill up your soul?

1. What is more important than food that can fill up your soul?

2. How much more do you pray and talk to God?

3. How do you make your relationship stronger with God?

• DAY 30 •

How does money change a person?

1 Timothy 6:10-

"For the love of money is the root of all evil: which while some coveted after, they have erred from the faith and pierced themselves through with sorrow."

In order to survive in life, I must work and have a job in order to have some income. If you want to have different things in life, you have to pay for them because things will not be given to you for free. Money can cause a lot of chaos and stress in a person's life. The love of money causes robberies and burglaries across the world.

Some people who are none believers of God don't want to see one person do better or succeed over them. One time a guy named Bill borrowed money from a friend. Bill who borrowed some money from his friend has the exact same job. Bill would always say that he clears more money than the person he borrowed money from, so where was his money going? The money was paid back, but the relationship fell apart over time. The guy would always say that the Lord would make a way and provide. We must have faith and believe in God, but God gives us common sense and knowledge on how to budget and spend accordingly. It's up to us on whether we use that knowledge or not. Bill borrowed money again from the same person, but never said a word of paying it back.

Bill didn't even say thank-you and stopped calling like he once did. The least Bill could have done was paid the money right back or decide not to accept the money.

How does money change a person?

1. How does money change a person?

2. Does money have an influence over how you act?

3. Have you noticed how many have changed a close friend or family member? How do you act toward that person?

• DAY 31 •

How do I maintain patience for the things I want?

Ecclesiastes 3:1-

"To everything there is a season, and a time to every purpose under heaven."

Your life is already planned out in the eyes of God. He knows the day that you will enter the Earth and the day that you will depart from your earthly home. Therefore, everything that happens in your life is not a surprise.

To our Almighty God, things that happen in our life can be seen as challenges or new opportunities. Sometimes, people try to plan things when it is not meant to be at that particular moment. You must follow the old saying of living one day at a time. Everything will happen in God's timing, not yours if you live a life close to God. A lot of couples' rush into a marriage and then move into a divorce. Several months later they get a divorce because it's not a part of God's timing.

Only if they would have waited and prayed a little more, they would have found out early on if it was meant to be. A guy wanted to marry a girl that he hadn't seen in over 12 years. The girl's response was let's date, get engaged, and then get married because a lot of things have changed in the course of 12 years. Sylvia already knew that he was involved in a relationship and had not fully ended the previous relationship. It was not God's timing for this to take place then the marriage wouldn't have lasted. Getting out of one relationship and then going full force into another one was not the correct route to go.

At least both parties realized it was not the right time for that. There were a lot of things both parties must work through in order to walk down the aisle. Maybe things will work out within the right season, but as for now, things are too complicated.

How do I maintain patience for the things I want?

1. How do I maintain patience for the things I want?

2. Have you ever rushed into doing something that you really wanted?

3. How do you feel when things don't go as you wanted them to?

• DAY 32 •

Why is telling the truth so important?

Ephesians 4:29-

"Let no corrupt communication proceed out of your mouth, but that which is good to use of edifying, that it may minister grace unto the hearers."

Is it worth telling the truth or sparing someone's feelings? A lot of people are untrustworthy. In our world today, you have to be careful of the people you trust both men and women. Be careful with the people who are constantly talking about the Bible and don't live a biblical life.

A lot of people can quote Bible Scriptures and tell others to be a good person, but he is not following through with what he is saying. In most cases, people cannot be honest. It is true what they say, what you do in the dark, will come to the light.

The internet is one of the most powerful weapons that can help you or destroy relationships. I have an experience of someone I deeply cared for that did nothing but lie, and the truth was exposed on the internet. It's wise to never go back in time from certain situations. If it didn't work out the first time due them not being trustworthy, then it's not going to work out the second time. He is not going to change because he doesn't want to be a better person.

When dealing with people, it's always best to be honest. God doesn't like liars, but through it all, he will always forgive us through our sins. Be cautious of what you say and how you treat people because you will reap what you sow. Remember that the way you handle situations will define your character, and as always, actions speak volumes.

Rachel once talked to Tom that claimed that the screen had stopped working on his phone. Rachel called Tom's number for a while and asked Tom was his phone working and he always told her no. After a while, Rachel called Tom's number from a different number and it rang. You see, Rachel communicated with Tom through social media.

Tom continued to say that his phone didn't work. So, Rachel got her friend's phone and sent a text message to Tom. He replied back to the text message identifying who he was and asking who had texted him. Now, this comes from Tom, a guy that Rachel cares a lot about, but why on Earth does he not want Rachel to call his phone anymore. Rachel knew that his phone worked, but wondered how long this was going to continue of him saying his phone doesn't work.

Tom should have told Rachel not to call his phone anymore, but instead he had to come up with the story of the screen had frozen and he only used the cell phone as an alarm clock, instead of being honest and telling the truth.

Why is telling the truth so important?

1. Why is telling the truth so important?

2. Have you ever been around a person who constantly lies all the time? How do you feel toward that person?

3. How do you treat a person who doesn't tell you the truth?

About the Author

Ann Rhodes was born and raised in a small city in Georgia. At the age of 8 years old, she started writing poetry by keeping it in a notebook. When she reached the sixth grade, it was the inspiration of her language arts teacher and her mother that encouraged her to share her poems. Her poems have been published by Channel 2 Action News, Poetry.com, and the local newspapers. In 2016, her first book of poetry was published "From the Beginning until Now". This poetry book contains poems that include reflections on life, spirituality, prayer, and influences that various people have had on her life. Her second poetry book that was released in 2019 titled "A Sight to Behold" continues poems about everlasting life and dealing with relationships.

I am currently an elementary school teacher in Georgia. I graduated from LaGrange College and Troy University with a degree in education. In my spare time, I enjoy writing, spending time with family, and being an inspiration to others.

Made in the USA
Columbia, SC
20 June 2023